01/18

Understanding
CREDIT AND DEBT

MONEY SKILLS
for KIDS

ROBYN HARDYMAN

PowerKiDS
press.
New York

Published in 2018 by **The Rosen Publishing Group, Inc.**
29 East 21st Street, New York, NY 10010

Cataloging-in-Publication Data
Names: Hardyman, Robyn.
Title: Understanding credit and debt / Robyn Hardyman.
Description: New York : PowerKids Press, 2018. | Series: Money skills for kids | Includes index.
Identifiers: ISBN 9781508153740 (pbk.) | ISBN 9781499434903 (library bound) | ISBN 9781499434804 (6 pack)
Subjects: LCSH: Consumer credit--Juvenile literature. | Debt--Juvenile literature. | Finance, Personal--Juvenile literature.
Classification: LCC HG3755.H349 2018 | DDC 332.024'02--dc23

Produced for Rosen by Calcium
Editors for Calcium: Sarah Eason and Jennifer Sanderson
Designers for Calcium: Paul Myerscough and Jennie Child
Picture researcher: Jennifer Sanderson

Photo Credits: Photo Credits: Cover: Getty: Kidstock. Inside: Shutterstock: Air Images 5, Andrey Arkusha 19, Andy Dean Photography 10, Antonio Guillem 17, Bacho 22, Danielfela 25, Diego Cervo 4, 31, Goodluz 11, Leonard Zhukovsky 13, Mangostock 16, Master L 23, Monkey Business Images 9, 15, Nenetus 27, Nevodka 7, Pressmaster 29, Rocketclips, Inc. 1, 21.

Manufactured in China.
CPSIA Compliance Information: Batch BS17PK: For Further Information contact Rosen Publishing, New York, New York at 1-800-237-9932.

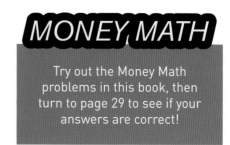

MONEY MATH

Try out the Money Math problems in this book, then turn to page 29 to see if your answers are correct!

CONTENTS

WHAT IS CREDIT? 4

FORMS OF CREDIT 6

BIG LOANS 8

MORTGAGES 10

NATIONAL DEBT 12

BIG BUSINESS 14

PERSONAL LOANS 16

PERSONAL DEBT 18

CREDIT CARDS 20

CREDIT AND DEBT 22

CREDIT SCORES 24

BAD DEBT 26

BE MONEY SMART 28

GLOSSARY 30

FURTHER READING 31

INDEX 32

WHAT IS CREDIT?

You probably already know that it's best to only buy things when you have enough money to pay for them. This is generally true. You should always try to buy things with money that is already yours. That means paying with cash or using a **debit card**, which takes your money from your bank account. Sometimes, though, it is not possible for adults to pay for all the things they need. That is where **credit** comes in.

BORROWING MONEY

Credit is borrowing money from a bank or a business and using it to buy things. People use credit when they do not have the whole amount needed to pay for something. This may be because the item they are buying is very expensive, such as a car or a house. It may also be because they are running low on money. Some people use credit to help them through a time when they do not have enough money. Perhaps they are between jobs, and their **income** is less than usual for a while. Perhaps they cannot work for a short time because they are sick or injured. In these situations, people use credit to pay for everyday **expenses**, such as rent and food.

Almost everyone will find they need to use credit at some time in their lives. Credit can be really useful, but it can cause problems if you're not careful. Some people get in the habit of using credit for things they want rather than need. They cannot really **afford** them, but the temptation is too great. They use credit to buy fashionable shoes, the newest video games, or to pay for expensive vacations. Regularly buying things that you cannot afford with credit can quickly lead to trouble.

We should try to avoid paying for everyday items with credit and use cash or our debit card if we can.

We often pay for more expensive things, such as vacations, using credit.

CREDIT IS NOT FREE MONEY

When you borrow from a bank or other lender to go shopping with credit, you have to pay an extra amount of money for the loan. This amount is called **interest**. It is how banks and lenders make money. For example, a bank lends you $100 but then charges you an extra $10 on top in interest. You pay the bank back $110, and the bank earns $10 from you. When a bank or lender makes millions of loans, it is called "big business."

Using credit can be really useful, but if you do not pay back your loans, you end up in **debt**. Being in debt means owing money, either to a person or a bank. The longer you do not pay back a loan, the worse it gets. This is because the lender continues to add interest to the amount you owe.

A LOT OF DEBT

The average American adult has more than $4,000 of debt on their **credit card**.

5

FORMS OF CREDIT

We are surrounded by temptation and advertisements urging us to spend money on more and more things. If we do not have enough money right now to pay for something, we can buy it on credit. Most people use credit to finance their lives. Usually, it is in a small way, but sometimes, people rely too much on credit. That is where the problems start.

FANTASTIC PLASTIC

For everyday spending, the most popular way to get credit is with a credit card. This allows you to buy things without using cash. You borrow the money from the bank that gives you the credit card. Each month, the bank sends you a **statement**, which tells you how much you owe. If you do not pay off the full amount, the bank adds interest to the amount you owe. Over time, this makes your debt even bigger. Many stores have credit cards of their own. You can use them to buy things in the store, and often they give you points for every dollar you spend. When you have earned a certain number of points, you get money off purchases or a free gift. It is a smart way to keep customers coming back.

Credit cards are useful for everyday spending, but what about more expensive items? To buy these, people can apply for a personal loan at a bank. If the bank agrees, the length of the loan and the amount of interest are set. This kind of loan is usually for a year or two, and the rates of interest can be very high. It is an expensive way to get credit.

BUCKS FOR BUSINESS

Businesses need loans, too. They usually need much larger amounts than individuals, because their projects are bigger and more complex. However, the same rules apply. The business must pay back an agreed amount each month. If it fails to keep up the payments, the lender can force its owners to sell the business to pay back the loan.

Credit cards are a handy way to pay for items in a store. Some have loyalty schemes that encourage you to use them whenever you purchase items.

THE FIRST CARD

The first-ever credit card was for the Diners Club. In 1949, Frank McNamara ate at a restaurant in New York but could not pay the bill because he had forgotten his wallet. This gave him the idea to set up the credit system called Diners Club. It is still going today.

BIG LOANS

Do you have dreams for your future? Do you see yourself as the next Bill Gates or Mark Zuckerberg? Do you want to have the best college education, so that you can contribute to solving some of the big problems in the world? Making dreams like these come true takes imagination, courage, and a lot of hard work. It also takes money.

SUCCESSFUL START-UPS

When you start a business, you have to hire people and find a place to work. You have to pay to produce the product or the service you are offering. You hope you will be making money soon, but at the beginning, your costs are high. A person starting a business will probably go to the bank for a loan. The bank will ask to see a detailed plan of the business, to see if it is worth risking their money. If they agree, they give the businessperson some start-up money. They agree on how long the loan will last and how much interest will be charged.

Some of the most familiar names in business today started out as small dreams. The owners were loaned start-up money, then their businesses grew strong and successful. Starbucks, the coffee chain, was started in 1971. Three friends—Jerry Baldwin, Zev Siegl, and Gordon Bowker—each borrowed some money and put $1,350 into developing their idea for selling coffee beans. Now Starbucks is worth billions of dollars!

Other businesses start with the help of **investors**. Maxine Clark started the famous toy store chain, Build-A-Bear. She used her own money to cover a lot of the start-up costs, but she knew she would need more help. Then two private investors supported her by buying 20% of her business for $4.5 million—all before the first store even opened! Clark's idea was so unique that the investors knew they would make money when the business became successful.

A GOOD INVESTMENT

A new business does have debt, but this is a positive kind of credit. It allows new ideas to flourish. This is similar to a young person taking out a loan to pay for their education. It is a good investment. A good education is likely to increase the young person's chances of getting a good job in the future, which will help them earn more money.

Borrowing money for your college education is a positive kind of debt, because it will give you better job opportunities in the future.

MONEY MATH

If ten people each borrow $10,000 from a bank to start their own business, how much does the bank lend altogether?

SEE PAGE 29 FOR THE ANSWER!

9

MORTGAGES

Usually, the biggest item a person will buy in their lifetime is a place to live. Whether it is an apartment or a mansion, buying a home is expensive. Very few people can afford the full price of a home when they buy it. They have to get a loan for some of the cost. Loans that are given to buy homes are called mortgages.

A LONG-TERM LOAN

People have to borrow a lot of money for a mortgage, so it takes a long time to pay off. A typical mortgage loan lasts for 30 years. That is almost as long as a person's entire working life. When you find a property you want to buy, you agree on a price with the person selling it. You then ask a bank or other lender for a mortgage. Banks will usually lend to you only if you already have some of the money you need. This is called your **deposit**. This is usually about 10% of the total cost of the home, but it could be more. Banks ask for this because they do not want to take the risk of the whole value of the property. If you fail to pay back the bank, it can take away your home. To earn back the money it loaned you, the bank will sell the property. If the price of property has fallen, it may get back less than it loaned.

A mortgage is often the biggest loan a person takes out in their lifetime.

If the lender agrees to give you a mortgage, it tells you how much interest they will charge you. The lender will calculate how much you need to repay each month. When the sale is complete, you give your deposit to the mortgage lender, and the mortgage lender gives the seller the rest of the agreed price. From then on, you must pay the lender the amount you have agreed to pay each month. This amount is usually made up of two parts—part of the total amount you borrowed and an amount of interest on top.

CHANGING INTEREST

Over the years, interest rates can change. When they go up, it is hard for people with a mortgage. They may have planned on paying a certain amount each month and think they can afford it. If interest rates go up a lot, their monthly mortgage payment goes up, too. This is why it is so important not to take out a mortgage bigger than one you can comfortably afford, even when interest rates are high.

The mortgage provider will explain the full terms of your loan to you.

ODD NAME

"Mortgage" is an odd name for a loan. The word comes from a term in an old version of the French language. It meant "death pledge." The debt, or pledge, "dies" when the full amount is paid off or when the person who took the loan fails to repay it.

NATIONAL DEBT

Sometimes, it is difficult to get through life without having to borrow money. We all have times when we cannot buy those big-ticket items on our own. Did you know that it is just the same for countries, too? Imagine what kind of expenses a whole country's government has. Sometimes, countries do not have enough money available to pay for all of those expenses. They need to borrow money, too. When a country does this, the amount it owes is called the national debt.

BIG BILLS

Running a country is expensive. There are roads and other transportation networks to build and maintain. There are hospitals and schools to run. The armed forces, police forces, firefighters, and many, many other government employees need to be paid. Just like individuals and families, countries are sometimes hit by nasty surprises that they need money for. Perhaps a natural disaster like an earthquake or flood causes millions of dollars of damage, and people need to be rescued and their homes rebuilt. Perhaps they go to war and have to pay for their armed forces to fight overseas. Although governments try to keep money in reserve, they never have enough to pay for everything.

BIG DEBT

The United States is like every other country. It has a huge national debt. In 2016, it was almost $19.5 trillion in debt. That is $19 with 12 zeros on the end! That is almost too big a number to understand. If you think of it as more than $60,000 for every single US citizen, you begin to get the picture. In the United Kingdom, the national debt is about $36,000 for every citizen. In Canada, it is about $22,000 for every citizen. In fact, there is a national debt crisis all around the world. Countries have too much debt, and they are not earning money fast enough to pay it off.

MONEY MATH

You run the government of a small country. Your national debt is $10 million. Every six months, the debt increases by $2 million. How much will your debt be after 18 months?

SEE PAGE 29 FOR THE ANSWER!

Disasters such as hurricanes and earthquakes cause damage to roads that governments have to pay to repair.

BIG BUSINESS

In addition to buying houses and running countries, credit is also used by businesses that are already operating. A business that is doing well may have ideas about how it can grow. It may need to borrow money on credit, so that it can take the next leap forward.

A GREAT IDEA

You have seen how important money is for starting a business. If your business is a success, you often need more money to make it grow. For example, if you start a jean business, you may have ten employees sewing jeans in a small workshop. When your jeans begin selling so well that your ten employees cannot make enough to supply all the stores that want them, you'll need to hire more people. Then you'll need to find a bigger factory and buy more sewing machines. All that requires money.

Business owners ask a bank or other lender for a loan so they can buy the things they need to make the business grow. The lender has a good look at the business to see if it will succeed in the future. If the lender agrees, it will lend the business the money, with interest. The loan is for less time than a mortgage. It may have to be repaid within a few years. The business will have to make enough money from its newly grown operation to pay back the loan, plus the interest. If it does not make enough and cannot repay the loan, the lender can close down the business.

Small businesses that are doing well often borrow money to help them grow.

BUYING BUSINESSES

Sometimes, a business will decide that the quickest way to grow the operation is to buy another complete business. For example, it is quicker to buy another business that makes jeans than it is to find a new factory and workers. When one business buys up another, it is called a takeover. Buying whole businesses is expensive, though. That is another reason why the buyer might ask for a loan from a lender.

BIG BUCKS

In 2014, Facebook bought the company that made the mobile messaging app WhatsApp. The deal was worth $19 billion.

PERSONAL LOANS

Sometimes, people take out a personal loan from a bank. This is usually for a particular project they have in mind, not just to contribute to their living expenses. It may be for purchasing a car, starting a building project, furnishing a home, or paying tuition fees for college.

SHOP AROUND

When people decide they need to take out a personal loan, it is important to shop around. As with every purchase we make, it is important to get the best value for our money. Lenders want new business, so they may offer terms that look attractive. Perhaps the interest rate is low for a period of time at the beginning, and a free gift is offered with every loan. The borrower should look carefully at these and think about the terms the lender is offering over the whole term of the loan. If the interest rate rises sharply after an initial low period, the loan may end up costing more overall. Personal loans can be very expensive.

Many adults receive a lot of mail from companies offering them personal loans. Usually, these companies want your business if you have a history of not paying off your credit cards in full. That means that you pay interest every month, which means the lender makes a profit. The smart thing to do is to stay focused and throw away this mail. Adults should only borrow money if they absolutely have to, and choose a lender that offers them the best terms. It can be tempting to take out more than one loan at a time, but adults can quickly find themselves in more debt than they can handle.

Many people take out a personal loan to buy a car.

Stay in control of your money by planning how you will pay off your loan each month.

PAYING OFF LOANS

When you take out a loan, make a plan of how you are going to pay it off. List your basic expenses each month, and add the monthly loan repayment to the list. Can you be sure you will have enough for the repayments? If not, do not borrow. You may have to give up some of the things you enjoy while you are paying off your loan. If you are borrowing to purchase a car or some other benefit you know you will enjoy, it makes it easier. Keep your goals in mind and stick to your plan. Personal loans are usually for a fairly short period of time—often a year or two—so it will not be long before you have paid off your debt.

MONEY MATH

You borrow $5,000 over two years. The interest rate is 20% and your monthly repayment is $250. How much will you have paid at the end of two years? The difference in the two amounts is the extra cost of borrowing the money.

SEE PAGE 29 FOR THE ANSWER!

PERSONAL DEBT

Imagine yourself as an adult. You have a checking account with the bank. Each month, your income is paid into it. You generally spend money using either a debit card or cash that you withdraw from an **ATM**. At the end of the month, your bank statement arrives in the mail. It tells you that you have gone into debt. You have a negative **balance**. How did that happen?

OVERDRAFTS

When you spend more money from your account than you have in it, you are in debt. You have what is called an **overdraft**. This can happen in several ways. Perhaps you wrote a **check** several weeks ago that you sent to someone, expecting them to cash it right away. They did not, and by the time they cashed it, you did not have enough in your account to cover it. Perhaps you went to the ATM and took money out of your account without checking that you had enough in it. You may have used your debit card too often. When this happens, the bank will react. It may refuse to make **transactions** on your account. That could mean that you cannot pay your bills. The bank will charge you a fee for your overdraft. This is usually an amount for each day that your account is overdrawn, and it can soon add up to a lot of money. Every day that you are overdrawn counts. If you fail to get your account out of the negative balance, the bank may close it down. You will also have a bad record that it will tell other banks about, so it could be hard for you to open an account at another bank or get loans.

OVERDRAFT PROTECTION

Banks do not like it when customers get overdrawn, but they understand that it can happen. When you open a checking account, you may be asked if you want debit overdraft protection. With this, if your account becomes overdrawn, the bank will automatically take money out of your savings account and put it into your checking account to cover bills. Banks charge a fee for this service.

STAY IN CREDIT

The best way to avoid overdrafts is to keep careful records. Make sure you know how much is in your account at all times. Record your checks, payments, and cash withdrawals.

An ATM is a handy way to withdraw money from your account, but remember to keep a record of how much you have taken out, so that you do not get overdrawn.

19

CREDIT CARDS

Credit cards allow you to buy things when you do not have the cash to pay for them. It is all about buying now and paying later. This may sound like a great idea, but it can land people in a lot of trouble.

HANDY MONEY

Credit cards can be useful if you need to spend money unexpectedly. For example, if your car breaks down and you do not have enough money in your bank account to pay for the repairs, you could pay for them using a credit card.

Banks give credit cards to their customers. You charge your purchases to the card. Each month, the bank sends you a statement telling you how much you have spent. If you pay off the full amount, there is no extra charge. Your balance is cleared, and you start again from zero the following month. If you do not pay off the full amount, the bank charges you interest on the amount you still owe. That is likely to be a high rate of interest, too. Then you make more purchases the following month, and the total you owe grows. Even more interest is charged on that higher amount, and so your debt begins to build up rapidly.

It is smart to pay off the full amount owed each month. If you cannot do that, you should pay off as much as you possibly can until the debt has been fully paid. This may mean managing without other things you would like for a while.

A SAFER WAY TO PAY

Credit cards are the best way to pay for things when you are shopping online. You enter the details of your credit card on the seller's site, and the purchase happens automatically. The banks that issue credit cards often promise to protect their customers if things go wrong with a purchase. For example, if you book a vacation online and pay for it, then the vacation company goes out of business before you travel, you cannot get your money back from that company. However, the credit card company might refund you the price you paid.

Credit cards are a safe way to pay for items when we shop online.

MONEY MATH

You have spent $100 on your credit card. Your interest rate is 20 percent every month. If you do not make any payment, how much will you owe on your card after the first month?

SEE PAGE 29 FOR THE ANSWER!

CREDIT AND DEBT

It is great for adults to have a credit card in their wallets for those times when they need it. However, these cards can be too much of a good thing. If we use them too often, we can get into too much debt.

A NATION IN DEBT

In 2015, Americans had a total of more than $900 billion of debt on their credit cards. That amount is increasing, too. It seems that we just cannot stop spending money we do not have. There are almost 600 million credit cards in use in the United States. That means that many people have more than one card. If you run up a large total on your credit card, each month, the bank needs a minimum payment to be made. As your total rises, so does the minimum payment. You just cannot find the cash for it, so what do you do? You get another credit card. You pay off the minimum amount on the first card using the second one, but now that one has debt, too. If you also use both cards for shopping, you are on your way to big trouble.

Credit card debt can become serious if you have more than one credit card.

Keep track of the interest rate you are paying on your credit card, and switch to a better deal if you can.

EXPENSIVE MONEY

You borrow $5,000 on a credit card with a typical rate of interest. The minimum payment is 2% each month. If you pay off only this minimum amount, it will take you 32 years to pay off the $5,000! You will also have paid an extra $7,789.56 in interest. So that $5,000 has cost you a total of $12,789.56!

NO INTEREST

Credit card companies try to attract customers by offering periods when no interest will be charged on the total you owe. This can be helpful, but it also encourages people to get more cards. The answer is not to spend more, but less, and to plan.

The best way to avoid getting in debt with credit cards is to plan ahead. That means making a **budget**. You make a list of all of your forms of income. Then you list all your basic expenses, or things you cannot manage without, such as rent, food, clothes, transportation costs, and so on.

If you have a credit card, the minimum monthly payment absolutely must be on this list. The difference between your expenses and your income is the amount you have to spend on nonessentials. The first nonessential you should spend on is the rest of the balance on your credit card. That is because you are paying interest on this amount, so it is costing you money. It is always better to spend any spare money on this, rather than saving it.

CREDIT SCORES

It is a good idea to pay back loans as fast as we can afford. We do not want to have debt hanging around us for years. We want to be free to move forward with our lives. There is another reason, though, why we should pay off our debts in full—our **credit score**.

KEEPING SCORE

Every time you take out a loan, whether it is with a credit card or a personal loan, the lender gathers information on how you pay it back. Over time, this information grows into a picture of how good you are as a borrower. The banks that lend to people are taking a risk when they lend to you. They need to know whether you are going to pay them back on time and in full, or if you are going to miss payments. If they never get their money back, it is bad business for them.

Lenders share this information with each other. They use it to calculate your credit score, or credit rating. If you have a history of making your payments on time, you will have a high score, which is good. If you regularly pay late or do not pay at all, you will have a lower score. Your score can matter. If you have a low credit score, you are less likely to receive a loan when you really need money for something important, such as a car, a mortgage, or your own business.

GET YOUR SCORE

When the time comes for you to think about taking out a loan, you can find out what your credit score is. The law says you are entitled to find out your own credit score free of charge from three different agencies, once a year. If there is information you think is wrong, you can challenge it. If you have a bad score, you can start to improve it. The best way to do that is to ensure that you make your payments on time and decrease your debt.

24

You will need to have a good credit score if you want to apply for a personal loan.

Your Credit Report

Credit Score:
Excellent

790

Commercial Loan Application

...designed to be completed by the applicant(s) with the Lender's assistance. Applicants should complete ..." or "Co-Borrower," as applicable. Borrower Co-Borrower Title will be held in what Name(s) Co- ...lso be provided (and the appropriate box checked) when the income or assets of a person ...the Borrower's spouse) will be used as a basis for loan qualification or the income or ...person who has community property rights pursuant to state law and ...

...formation; therefore, it must be true, complet... ...of your application before accepting d... ...ay seek information from other...

MONEY MATH

Credit scores usually range from 300 to 850. What is the score in the middle of this range?

SEE PAGE 29 FOR THE ANSWER!

BAD DEBT

Sometimes, debt problems can get out of control. People spend more than they can afford, build up big bills on credit cards, and reach a point where they just cannot see how they will ever get out of debt. Fortunately, help is at hand.

GET HELP

The US government has a counseling service for people with debt problems. The service has many ways to help people manage their money. It can help with planning a budget to take you forward, so that you stop spending more than you have. It can put together a realistic plan for paying off your debt. This will be a slow and steady process, because it can take a long time to clear big debts. The plan will be tailored to your individual needs, since everyone's situation is different.

UNDERSTANDING

Lenders are also there to help with debt problems. They understand that sometimes things happen to people that they could not have expected. Perhaps someone has lost their job or has gotten sick. These unpleasant surprises affect people's ability to pay what they owe. The bank will sit down with them and figure out a plan for making regular payments. If people show that they are serious about sticking to this plan, lenders may not take drastic steps against them, such as taking away someone's home or other belongings.

BE SMART

When we are spending more than we earn, there are two main ways out of the problem. We can spend less, or we can earn more. These are the first things to try to fix if you find yourself overspending. Could you get another job or one that pays better? Look at your spending very carefully. There are almost always things you can cut back on. It may not be much fun for a while, but the satisfaction you get when you are finally debt-free will make it worthwhile. Finally, if you are tempted by the credit card in your wallet, consider cancelling it. If it is not there, you cannot use it. Get in the habit of knowing how much you have to spend, and shop with cash or your debit card whenever you can.

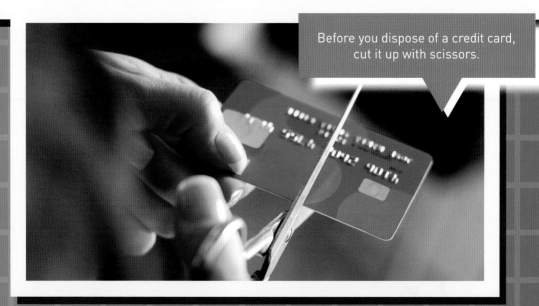

Before you dispose of a credit card, cut it up with scissors.

BANKRUPTCY

When people have so much debt that they could not ever pay it off, they can choose to apply for **bankruptcy** as a last resort. Bankruptcy can give you a fresh start. You must sell everything you own to pay off as much as you can. What you cannot pay is wiped off your record. However, this is not an easy option. Bankruptcy information stays on your record for a long time, and it will be hard to get credit again in the future.

BE MONEY SMART

We have seen that credit is a useful way to borrow money for a short time, until you have enough to pay back the loan. Borrowing money can be a positive step toward achieving our goals. However, it can also lead to the bad kind of debt, the kind where our spending is out of control. To use credit well, we need to be smart.

BE IN CONTROL

The trick with credit is to make it work for you. Stay in control of it, rather than letting it control your life. That means knowing how much you can afford to borrow. Make a budget, and stick to it. Whenever you can, pay for things with cash or your debit card. Sometimes you will have extra expenses — for example, when you buy gifts around holidays. You could purchase those extra things on a credit card, as long as you know that you can pay off the cost in a short amount of time. The number one rule is to pay off the minimum amount each month, no matter what. After that, pay off as much as you can possibly afford. Ideally, pay off the full amount each month. That way, the loan is costing you nothing.

Being smart about credit also means doing your research. There are many lenders out there, and they charge different rates of interest. Find the deals that work best for you. Remember that an interest-free period may not be the best deal, especially if the rate then goes sky-high for the rest of the loan period.

EARN RESPECT

Get into the habit of paying off your debts quickly, even if the amounts are very small. If a friend at school lends you a dollar to buy a cookie, remember to take a dollar to school the next day to pay them back. If your mom lends you some money to help you buy something you are saving up for, keep a record of how much you owe, and pay her back in small amounts when you can. You will find that if you do this, people will be more willing to lend you money next time! Nobody wants to lend to someone who never repays them.

Use credit wisely and only when you really have to. Think twice before you reach for the plastic in your wallet.

MONEY MATH ANSWERS

Page 9: The bank lends $100,000.
Page 13: After 18 months, your debt is $16 million.
Page 17: You will have paid $6,000.
Page 21: You owe $120.
Page 25: The middle score is 575.

GLOSSARY

afford To have enough money to pay for something.

ATM Short for Automated Teller Machine, a machine that allows bank customers to take money out of their account.

balance The amount of money in an account.

bankruptcy Being in debt and unable to cover the debt.

budget A detailed plan of how to spend money.

check A printed form on which you write instructions to your bank to pay money from your account.

credit Borrowing money to pay for something.

credit card A plastic card from a bank that allows customers to borrow money to pay for things.

credit score A rating of how good a borrower you are.

debit card A plastic card from a bank that allows customers to pay for things using money from their own checking account.

debt An amount of money owed to someone else.

deposit An amount of money you pay toward an expensive purchase.

expenses Money we spend.

income Money that is earned from work, investments, and business.

interest Money paid by people who borrow money, to the people who lend it to them.

investor A person who puts money into a business with the hope that the business will grow in value and make them more money.

overdraft When you take more money out of your bank account than it has in it.

statement A printed list of money that has gone into and out of an account in a period of time.

transactions Activity of money going into and out of an account.

FURTHER READING

BOOKS

Marsico, Katie. *Using Credit Wisely*. Cherry Lake Publishing, 2015.

McGillian, Jamie Kyle. *The Kids' Money Book*. Sterling Children's Books, 2016.

Nourigat, Paul. *Debt Dangers*. Far Beyond Publishing, 2014.

WEBSITES

Due to the changing nature of Internet links, PowerKids Presshas developed an online list of websites related to the subjectof this book. This site is updated regularly. Please use this linkto access the list:

www.powerkidslinks.com/msfk/credit

31

INDEX

B
balance, 18, 20, 23
Baldwin, Jerry, 8
bank account, 4, 20
Bowker, Gordon, 8
budget, 23, 26, 28
Build-A-Bear, 8

C
cash, 4, 6, 18–20, 22, 27–28
Clark, Maxine, 8
credit card, 5–7, 16, 20–24, 26–28
credit score, 24–25

D
debit card, 4, 18
deposit, 10–11
Diners Club, 7

E
expenses, 4, 12, 16–17, 23, 28

G
Gates, Bill, 8

I
income, 4, 18, 23

interest, 5–6, 8, 11, 14, 16–17, 20–21, 23, 28
investors, 8

L
loans, 5, 6, 8, 10–11, 14–18, 24, 28

M
McNamara, Frank, 7
mortgages, 10–11, 14, 24

N
national debt, 12–13

O
overdraft protection, 18
overdrafts, 18

S
Siegl, Zev, 8
Starbucks, 8
statement, 6, 18, 20

Z
Zuckerberg, Mark, 8